delectable and delicious

quick noodles

Consultant Editor:
Valerie Ferguson

HERMES
HOUSE

Contents

Introduction   4

Types of Noodles   6

Techniques   8

Stir-fried Noodles   10

Hot & Spicy   20

East Meets West   30

Noodle Soups   40

Vegetarian Noodles   52

Introduction

Noodles must be the original fast food. Their history goes back thousands of years and they are loved the world over, but this book concentrates on the noodle dishes of Asia.

Unlike Italian pasta, which is produced almost exclusively from wheat, Asian noodles are made from a variety of grains, including buckwheat and rice, and are often enriched with egg. They may also be of vegetable origin: cellophane noodles are made from mung beans, and soya beans, chick-peas and even seaweed are just some of the sources of the hundreds of different varieties now available.

For both everyday family meals and entertaining, noodles are an excellent choice. They combine brilliantly with all kinds of vegetables, fish, poultry and meat and happily absorb any flavours that are thrown at them, whether mild, fragrant, sweet, sour, salty or spicy-hot. Perfect for the swiftest of stir-fries, they also make superb soups, which can be light and delicate or hearty main courses, with the stock serving merely to moisten the dish.

Noodle dishes provide the ideal opportunity to experiment and become familiar with a wide range of oriental ingredients and to discover a wonderful world of flavour.

Types of Noodles

The range of Asian noodles, both fresh and dried, is extensive.

Cellophane Noodles

Sometimes sold as transparent, glass or bean thread noodles, these thin, clear, shiny noodles are generally made from mung bean flour. The dried types are soaked in hot water before cooking. Unlike some Oriental noodles, cellophane noodles can be reheated successfully after cooking, and are a favourite ingredient of stir-fries.

Cellophane Noodles

Egg Noodles

Available in skeins or bundles, egg noodles are widely used throughout Asia, and range from very thin strands (vermicelli) to narrow ribbons. They are made from wheat with added egg, giving the characteristic yellow colour. Japanese egg noodles, known as ramen, are usually sold in coils or blocks. They are the closest in texture and flavour to Italian pasta.

Egg Noodles

Rice Noodles

Made from rice flour and water, the dried version comes in long strands in various thicknesses, ranging from very thin to wide ribbons and sheets, and are usually sold in neat bundles, tied with raffia. Fresh rice noodles are also available. Rinse rice noodles in warm water and drain before use. Rice noodles are traditionally served at Chinese birthday celebrations; the longer the strands, the more auspicious the omens for a long and healthy life.

Rice Noodles

Japanese Rice Noodles

Rice Vermicelli

Thin, white and brittle, rice vermicelli is sold in large bundles. When pre-soaked and drained, it cooks almost instantly in hot liquid. Small quantities of rice vermicelli can also be deep-fried straight from the packet to make a crisp garnish for a soup or a sauce dish.

Rice Vermicelli

Soba Noodles

These Japanese
noodles are
made from
buckwheat
flour (or a
mixture of
buckwheat
and wheat
flour) and are

Soba Noodles

traditionally cooked in simmering
water. Thin and brownish in colour,
flavoursome and quite chewy, they
may be served either hot or cold, with
garnishes and a dipping
sauce. There is also a dark
green variety called
cha-soba (tea
soba), which
is made of
buckwheat
and green tea. *Green Soba Noodles*

Somen Noodles

Wheat flour is used to make these
delicate white Japanese
noodles. Like
vermicelli,
they will
cook very
quickly in
boiling
water. Somen
noodles are sold in dried *Somen Noodles*
form, usually tied in
bundles that are held
together with a paper band.
They are ideal in soups and one-pot
meals and are often served cold
as a summer dish.

Udon Noodles

Thick and starchy, these popular and
versatile Japanese noodles are similar to
Italian pasta and can be substituted for
linguine. Made
from wheat
flour and
water, they
are usually
round in
shape and
are more
substantial
than somen noodles. *Udon Noodles*
A dried wholewheat
version is available in some wholefood
shops. Udon are also sold fresh, in
chilled vacuum packs, or pre-cooked.
They are generally served in hot
soups, such as Udon Pot. They are also
frequently used in mixed meat and
vegetable dishes.

Instant Noodles

Packets of pre-cooked egg noodles are
a familiar sight in
the West. They
come in a
wide range
of flavourings,
such as
chicken,
prawn and
beef, and make
a convenient
stand-by when time
is very limited. *Instant Noodles*

7

Techniques

Storing Noodles

Store dried noodles in the original packaging in airtight containers in a cool, dry place. They will stay fresh for many months. Fresh noodles (available from the chilled cabinets in Oriental food stores) keep for several days in the fridge if sealed in the plastic bag in which they were bought. Check use-by dates. Fresh egg noodles can be frozen successfully.

Preparing Noodles

Some noodles, notably cellophane noodles and rice noodles, must be soaked in hot water and drained before use. Follow the instructions in individual recipes. Noodles that are to be cooked twice (par-boiled, then stir-fried or simmered in sauce) are initially cooked until they are barely tender, then drained, refreshed under cold running water, and drained again. If appropriate, they may be tossed with a little oil to prevent any strands from sticking together. At this stage they can be stored in an airtight container in the fridge for several days.

Cooking Noodles

Add noodles to a large saucepan of rapidly boiling water (lightly salted if you wish), and cook for the time recommended on the packet. Unlike Italian pasta, which should retain a bit of bite, Oriental noodles are cooked until they are tender. Try to avoid overcooking, however, which can make them soggy.

Frying Noodles

Dried noodles are sometimes fried for garnishing or for use as a noodle cake. In this case, do not pre-cook the noodles.

Stir-frying Techniques

Have the required ingredients ready-prepared before cooking.

1 Heat an empty wok over a high heat. This prevents food sticking and will ensure an even heat. Add the oil and swirl it around so that it coats the base and halfway up the sides of the heated wok.

2 Add the ingredients, starting with the aromatics (garlic, ginger, spring onions). It is important that the oil is hot enough so that when food is added it will start to cook immediately, but do not wait for the oil to get so hot that it is almost smoking or the aromatics will burn and become bitter. Toss the aromatics in the oil for a few seconds.

3 Now add the main ingredients that require longer cooking, such as dense vegetables or meat, followed by the faster-cooking items. Toss and turn the ingredients from the centre of the wok to the sides.

Making Chicken Stock

Home-made chicken stock makes the world of difference to noodle soup.

1 Put about 1.6 kg/3½ lb meaty chicken bones into a large saucepan, add 3 litres/5 pints/13 cups water and slowly bring to the boil, skimming off any foam. Add two slices of fresh root ginger, two garlic cloves, two celery sticks, four spring onions, a handful of fresh coriander stalks and about 10 crushed peppercorns.

2 Reduce the heat and simmer the stock for 2–2½ hours. Remove from the heat and leave to cool, uncovered and undisturbed. Strain into a clean bowl, leaving the last dregs behind as they tend to cloud the soup. Use as required, discarding any fat that congeals on top.

Soft Fried Noodles

A very basic dish for serving as an accompaniment or light meal.

Serves 4–6

INGREDIENTS
350 g/12 oz dried egg noodles
30 ml/2 tbsp vegetable oil
30 ml/2 tbsp finely chopped
　spring onions
soy sauce, to taste
salt and freshly ground
　black pepper

1 Cook the noodles in a saucepan of boiling water until they are just tender, following the instructions on the packet. Drain, rinse them under cold running water and then drain again thoroughly.

2 Heat the oil in a wok or frying pan and swirl it around. Add the chopped spring onions and fry for 30 seconds. Add the noodles, stirring gently to separate the strands.

3 Reduce the heat and fry the noodles until they are heated through, lightly browned and crisp on the outside, but still soft inside. Season with soy sauce, salt and pepper. Serve at once.

Right: Soft Fried Noodles (top);
Egg Fried Noodles

Egg Fried Noodles

Yellow bean sauce gives these noodles a savoury flavour.

Serves 4–6

INGREDIENTS
60 ml/4 tbsp vegetable oil
4 spring onions, cut into 1 cm/½ in rounds
350 g/12 oz medium-thick egg noodles,
　cooked until just tender
juice of 1 lime
15 ml/1 tbsp soy sauce
2 garlic cloves, finely chopped
175 g/6 oz chicken breast, thinly sliced
175 g/6 oz raw prawns, peeled and deveined
175 g/6 oz squid, cleaned and cut into rings
15 ml/1 tbsp yellow bean sauce
15 ml/1 tbsp Thai fish sauce *(nam pla)*
15 ml/1 tbsp soft light brown sugar
2 eggs
fresh coriander leaves, to garnish

1 Heat half the oil in a wok or large frying pan. Add the spring onions, stir-fry for 2 minutes, then add the noodles, lime juice and soy sauce and stir-fry for 2–3 minutes. Transfer to a bowl and keep warm.

2 Heat the remaining oil and stir-fry the garlic, chicken, prawns and squid over a high heat until cooked. Stir in the yellow bean sauce, fish sauce and sugar, then break in the eggs, stirring until set. Add the noodles and heat through. Garnish with coriander.

Special Chow Mein

Lap cheong, a delicious air-dried Chinese sausage, available from most Chinese supermarkets, brings extra flavour to this classic noodle dish.

Serves 4–6

INGREDIENTS
450 g/1 lb egg noodles
45 ml/3 tbsp vegetable oil
2 garlic cloves, sliced
5 ml/1 tsp chopped fresh root ginger
1 red chilli, seeded and chopped
2 *lap cheong*, about 75 g/3 oz, rinsed and
    sliced, or diced ham or salami
1 boneless chicken breast,
    thinly sliced
16 raw tiger prawns, peeled, tails left intact
    and deveined
115 g/4 oz/¾ cup green beans
225 g/8 oz/1 cup beansprouts
50 g/2 oz garlic chives
30 ml/2 tbsp soy sauce
15 ml/1 tbsp oyster sauce
15 ml/1 tbsp sesame oil
salt and freshly ground black pepper
2 spring onions, shredded,
    and 15 ml/1 tbsp coriander leaves,
    to garnish

1 Cook the noodles in a saucepan of boiling water, following the instructions on the packet, until just tender. Drain well and set aside.

COOK'S TIP: Garlic or Chinese chives have larger leaves than ordinary chives and have a mild garlic flavour.

2 Heat 15 ml/1 tbsp of the oil in a wok or large frying pan and fry the garlic, ginger and chilli. Add the *lap cheong* (or ham or salami), chicken, prawns and green beans. Stir-fry for about 2 minutes over a high heat or until the chicken and prawns are cooked. Transfer the mixture to a bowl and set aside.

3 Heat the remaining oil in the same wok. Add the beansprouts and garlic chives. Stir fry for 1–2 minutes.

4 Add the noodles and toss and stir to mix. Season with soy sauce, oyster sauce, salt and pepper.

5 Return the prawn mixture to the wok. Reheat and mix well with the noodles. Stir in the sesame oil. Serve garnished with spring onions and coriander leaves.

Thai Fried Noodles

This stir-fried dish, made with rice noodles, is considered one of the national dishes of Thailand and has a fascinating flavour and texture.

Serves 4–6

INGREDIENTS
350 g/12 oz rice noodles
45 ml/3 tbsp vegetable oil
15 ml/1 tbsp chopped garlic
16 raw king prawns, peeled, tails left intact
   and deveined
2 eggs, lightly beaten
15 ml/1 tbsp dried shrimps, rinsed
30 ml/2 tbsp pickled mooli
50 g/2 oz fried beancurd, cut into
   small slivers
2.5 ml/½ tsp dried chilli flakes
115 g/4 oz garlic chives, cut into
   5 cm/2 in lengths
225 g/8 oz/1 cup beansprouts
50 g/2 oz/½ cup roughly chopped
   roasted peanuts
5 ml/1 tsp granulated sugar
15 ml/1 tbsp dark soy sauce
30 ml/2 tbsp Thai fish sauce
30 ml/2 tbsp tamarind juice
30 ml/2 tbsp coriander leaves and kaffir
   lime wedges, to garnish

1 Soak the noodles in warm water for 20 minutes. Drain and set aside. Heat 15 ml/1 tbsp of the oil in a wok or large frying pan. Add the garlic and stir-fry until golden. Stir in the prawns and stir-fry for 1–2 minutes. Remove from the wok and set aside.

2 Heat another 15 ml/1 tbsp of oil in the wok. Add the eggs and tilt the wok to spread them into a thin sheet. Stir to scramble and break the egg into small pieces. Remove from the wok and set aside with the prawns.

3 Heat the remaining oil in the wok. Add the dried shrimps, pickled mooli, beancurd and dried chillies. Stir briefly. Add the soaked noodles and stir-fry for 5 minutes.

4 Add the garlic chives, half the beansprouts and half the peanuts. Season with the sugar, soy sauce, fish sauce and tamarind juice. Mix well and then cook until the noodles are heated through.

COOK'S TIP: Dried shrimps are small peeled shrimps that have been salted and dried in the sun. They have a strong fishy taste and are used to season Oriental dishes.

5 Return the prawn and egg mixture to the wok and mix with the noodles. Serve garnished with the remaining beansprouts and peanuts, the coriander leaves and lime wedges.

15

Five-flavour Noodles

Despite its name this is a versatile dish and you can add as many different ingredients as you wish to make an exciting and tasty stir-fry.

Serves 4

INGREDIENTS
300 g/11 oz dried thin egg
    noodles or 500 g/1¼ lb fresh
    soba noodles
200 g/7 oz lean boneless pork
22.5 ml/4½ tsp sunflower oil
10 g/¼ oz grated fresh root ginger
1 garlic clove, crushed
200 g/7 oz/1½ cups roughly chopped
    green cabbage
115 g/4 oz/½ cup beansprouts
1 green pepper, seeded and cut into
    fine strips
1 red pepper, seeded and cut into
    fine strips
salt and freshly ground
    black pepper
20 ml/4 tsp *ao-nori* seaweed,
    to garnish (optional)

FOR THE SEASONING MIX
60 ml/4 tbsp Worcestershire sauce
15 ml/1 tbsp soy sauce
15 ml/1 tbsp oyster sauce
15 ml/1 tbsp sugar
2.5 ml/½ tsp salt
freshly ground white pepper

1 Cook the noodles following the instructions on the packet until just tender. Drain well and set aside. Cut the pork into 3–4 cm/1¼–1½ in strips and season with salt and pepper.

2 Heat 7.5 ml/1½ tsp of the oil in a large wok or frying pan. Stir-fry the pork until just cooked, then remove it from the pan.

3 Wipe the wok with kitchen paper and heat the remaining oil in it. Add the ginger, garlic and cabbage and stir-fry for 1 minute.

4 Add the beansprouts, stir until softened, then add the strips of red and green pepper and stir-fry the mixture for 1 minute more.

5 Return the pork to the pan and add the noodles. Stir in all the ingredients for the seasoning mix and stir-fry for 2–3 minutes. Serve immediately, sprinkled with *ao-nori* seaweed, if using.

COOK'S TIP: *Ao-nori* is a flaked, dried green seaweed, available from Oriental food stores.

Stir-fried Rice Noodles with Chicken & Prawns

Shellfish has a natural affinity with both meat and poultry. This Thai-style recipe has the characteristic sweet, sour and salty flavour.

Serves 4

INGREDIENTS
225 g/8 oz dried flat rice noodles
120 ml/4 fl oz/½ cup water
60 ml/4 tbsp Thai fish sauce (*nam pla*)
15 ml/1 tbsp sugar
15 ml/1 tbsp lime juice
5 ml/1 tsp paprika
pinch of cayenne pepper
45 ml/3 tbsp oil
2 garlic cloves, finely chopped
1 skinless, boneless chicken breast, finely sliced
8 raw prawns, peeled, deveined and cut in half
1 egg
50 g/2 oz/½ cup coarsely crushed roasted peanuts
3 spring onions, cut into short lengths
175 g/6 oz/¾ cup beansprouts
fresh coriander leaves and 1 lime, cut into wedges, to garnish

1 Place the noodles in a bowl, cover with warm water and soak for 30 minutes. Drain. Combine the water, fish sauce, sugar, lime juice, paprika and cayenne in a bowl. Set aside.

2 Heat the oil in a wok. Fry the garlic for 30 seconds. Add the chicken and prawns. Stir-fry for 3–4 minutes.

3 Push the chicken and prawn mixture in the wok out to the sides. Break the egg into the centre, then quickly stir to break up the yolk and cook over a medium heat until the egg is just lightly scrambled.

4 Add the drained noodles and the fish sauce mixture to the wok. Mix together well. Add half the crushed peanuts and cook, stirring frequently, until the noodles are soft and most of the liquid has been absorbed.

5 Add the spring onions and half the beansprouts. Cook, stirring for 1 minute more. Spoon on to a platter. Sprinkle with the remaining peanuts and beansprouts. Garnish with the coriander and lime wedges and serve.

COOK'S TIP: Thai fish sauce, or *nam pla*, is made from anchovies. It is at its best when recently made: avoid very dark brown sauce, which will be too old.

Lemon Grass Prawns on Crisp Noodle Cake

A creamy sauce with a kick from hot chillies coats these prawns.

Serves 4

INGREDIENTS

300 g/11 oz thin egg noodles
60 ml/4 tbsp vegetable oil
500 g/1¼ lb medium raw king prawns,
　peeled and deveined
2.5 ml/½ tsp ground coriander
15 ml/1 tbsp ground turmeric
2 garlic cloves, finely chopped
2 slices fresh root ginger, finely chopped
2 lemon grass stalks, finely chopped
2 shallots, finely chopped
15 ml/1 tbsp tomato purée
250 ml/8 fl oz/1 cup coconut cream
15–30 ml/1–2 tbsp fresh lime juice
15–30 ml/1–2 tbsp Thai fish sauce (*nam pla*)
4–6 kaffir lime leaves (optional)
1 cucumber, peeled, seeded and cut into
　5 cm/2 in batons
1 tomato, seeded and cut into strips
2 red chillies, seeded and finely sliced
salt and freshly ground black pepper
2 spring onions, finely sliced, and a few
　fresh coriander sprigs, to garnish

1 Cook the egg noodles in a saucepan of boiling water until just tender. Drain, rinse under cold running water and drain well. Heat 15 ml/1 tbsp of the oil in a large frying pan. Add the noodles, coating them evenly, and fry for 4–5 minutes until crisp and golden.

2 Turn the noodle cake over and fry the other side. Alternatively, make four individual cakes. Keep hot.

3 In a bowl, toss the prawns with the ground coriander, turmeric, garlic, ginger and lemon grass. Add salt and pepper to taste.

4 Heat the remaining oil in a large frying pan. Add the chopped shallots, fry them for 1 minute, then add the prawns and fry for 2 minutes more. Using a slotted spoon, remove the prawns from the pan.

5 Stir the tomato purée and coconut cream into the mixture remaining in the pan. Stir in lime juice and fish sauce to taste. Bring the sauce to a simmer, return the prawns, then add the kaffir lime leaves, if using, and the cucumber. Simmer gently until the prawns are cooked and the sauce is reduced to a coating consistency.

6 Add the tomato, stir until just warmed through, then add the chillies. Serve on top of the crisp noodle cake(s), garnished with sliced spring onions and coriander sprigs.

Singapore Rice Vermicelli

Simple and speedily prepared, this lightly curried rice noodle dish is a full and satisfying meal in a bowl.

Serves 4

INGREDIENTS

225 g/8 oz dried rice vermicelli
15 ml/1 tbsp vegetable oil
1 egg, lightly beaten
2 garlic cloves, finely chopped
2 large red or green chillies, seeded and
    finely chopped
15 ml/1 tbsp medium curry powder
1 red pepper, seeded and thinly sliced
1 green pepper, seeded and thinly sliced
1 carrot, cut into matchsticks
1.5 ml/¼ tsp salt
60 ml/4 tbsp vegetable stock
115 g/4 oz cooked peeled prawns,
    thawed if frozen
75 g/3 oz lean ham, cut into
    1 cm/½ in cubes
15 ml/1 tbsp light soy sauce

2 Heat 5 ml/1 tsp of the oil in a non-stick frying pan or wok. Add the egg and scramble until set. Remove with a slotted spoon and set aside. Wipe the pan with kitchen paper.

3 Heat the remaining oil in the clean pan. Stir-fry the garlic and chillies for a few seconds, then stir in the curry powder. Cook for 1 minute, stirring, then add the vegetables and stock.

1 Soak the vermicelli in a bowl of boiling water for 4 minutes or following the instructions on the packet. Drain them thoroughly and set them aside.

4 Bring to the boil. Add the prawns, ham, scrambled egg, rice vermicelli and soy sauce. Mix well. Cook, stirring, until all the liquid has been absorbed and the mixture is hot. Serve at once.

Clay Pot of Chilli Squid & Noodles

Light, smooth-textured noodles, succulent squid and a medley of crisp vegetables are perfectly complemented by this hot, spicy sauce.

Serves 4

INGREDIENTS
675 g/1½ lb squid
30 ml/2 tbsp vegetable oil
3 slices fresh root ginger, finely shredded
2 garlic cloves, finely chopped
1 red onion, finely sliced
1 carrot, finely sliced
1 celery stick, diagonally sliced
50 g/2 oz sugar snap peas, topped
    and tailed
5 ml/1 tsp sugar
15 ml/1 tbsp chilli bean paste
2.5 ml/½ tsp chilli powder
75 g/3 oz cellophane noodles, soaked in
    hot water until soft
120 ml/4 fl oz/½ cup Chicken Stock
    or water
15 ml/1 tbsp soy sauce
15 ml/1 tbsp oyster sauce
5 ml/1 tsp sesame oil
pinch of salt
fresh coriander leaves,
    to garnish

1 Prepare the squid. Holding the body in one hand, gently pull away the head and tentacles. Discard the head; trim and reserve the tentacles. Remove the transparent "quill" from inside the body of the squid. Peel off the brown skin on the outside of the body.

2 Rub a little salt into the squid and wash thoroughly under cold running water. Cut the body of the squid into rings or split it open lengthways, score criss-cross patterns on the inside of the body and cut it into 5 x 4 cm/ 2 x 1½ in pieces.

3 Heat the oil in a large clay pot or flameproof casserole. Add the shredded ginger, garlic and onion and fry for 1–2 minutes. Add the squid, carrot, celery and sugar snap peas. Fry until the squid curls up. Season with salt and sugar and stir in the chilli bean paste and chilli powder. Transfer the mixture to a bowl and set aside.

4 Drain the soaked noodles and add them to the clay pot or casserole. Stir in the stock or water, soy sauce and oyster sauce. Cover and cook over a medium heat for about 10 minutes or until the noodles are tender.

5 Return the squid and vegetables to the pot. Cover and cook for about 5–6 minutes more until all the flavours are combined.

6 Just before serving, taste and adjust the seasoning as necessary. Drizzle with the sesame oil and sprinkle with the coriander leaves.

Crispy Fried Rice Vermicelli

A crunchy tangle of noodles with pork and prawns tossed in a sauce that combines sweet, sour, salty and hot flavours.

Serves 4–6

INGREDIENTS
oil, for frying
175 g/6 oz rice vermicelli
15 ml/1 tbsp chopped garlic
4–6 dried chillies, seeded and chopped
30 ml/2 tbsp chopped shallot
15 ml/1 tbsp dried shrimps, rinsed
115 g/4 oz minced pork
115 g/4 oz raw prawns, peeled and chopped
30 ml/2 tbsp brown bean sauce
30 ml/2 tbsp rice wine vinegar
45 ml/3 tbsp Thai fish sauce *(nam pla)*
75 g/3 oz palm sugar
30 ml/2 tbsp tamarind water or lime juice
115 g/4 oz/½ cup beansprouts

FOR THE GARNISH
2 spring onions, shredded
30 ml/2 tbsp fresh coriander leaves
2 heads pickled garlic
2-egg omelette, rolled and sliced
2 red chillies, chopped

1 Heat the oil in a wok. Break the rice vermicelli apart into small handfuls about 7.5 cm/3 in long. Deep-fry in the hot oil until they puff up. Remove and drain on kitchen paper.

2 Pour most of the oil from the wok, leaving 30 ml/2 tbsp. Add the garlic, chillies, shallot and dried shrimps to the wok and fry until fragrant.

3 Add the minced pork and stir-fry for about 3–4 minutes until it is no longer pink. Add the prawns and fry for a further 2 minutes. Remove the mixture from the wok and set aside.

4 Add the brown bean sauce, vinegar, fish sauce and palm sugar to the wok. Bring to a gentle boil, stir to dissolve the sugar and cook until the mixture is thick and syrupy.

5 Add the tamarind water or lime juice and adjust the seasoning: it should be sweet, sour and salty. Reduce the heat. Add the pork and prawn mixture and the beansprouts to the sauce; stir until heated through.

COOK'S TIP: Pickled garlic and tamarind are available from Oriental stores. To make tamarind water, soak about 15 ml/1 tbsp tamarind pulp in 60 ml/4 tbsp hot water for 10 minutes, then strain.

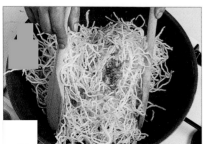

6 Add the rice noodles and toss gently to coat them with the sauce without breaking the noodles too much. Transfer to a platter and garnish with spring onions, coriander leaves, pickled garlic, omelette strips and red chillies. Serve immediately.

27

Rice Noodles with Beef & Black Bean Sauce

This is an excellent combination – beef with a hot chilli sauce tossed with silky smooth rice noodles.

Serves 4

INGREDIENTS
450 g/1 lb fresh broad rice noodles
60 ml/4 tbsp vegetable oil
1 onion, finely sliced
2 garlic cloves, finely chopped
2 slices fresh root ginger,
    finely chopped
225 g/8 oz mixed peppers, seeded and
    cut into strips
350 g/12 oz rump steak, finely sliced
    against the grain
45 ml/3 tbsp fermented black beans,
    rinsed in warm water, drained
    and chopped
30 ml/2 tbsp soy sauce
30 ml/2 tbsp oyster sauce
15 ml/1 tbsp chilli black
    bean sauce
15 ml/1 tbsp cornflour
120 ml/4 fl oz/½ cup stock or water
2 spring onions, finely chopped,
    and 2 red chillies, seeded and
    finely sliced, to garnish

1 Rinse the noodles in hot water. Drain well and set aside. Heat half the oil in a wok or large frying pan, swirling it around. Add the onion, garlic, ginger and mixed peppers. Stir-fry for 3–5 minutes, then remove with a slotted spoon and keep hot.

2 Add the remaining oil to the wok. When hot, add the sliced beef and fermented black beans and stir-fry over a high heat for 5 minutes or until they are cooked.

3 In a small bowl, blend the soy sauce, oyster sauce and chilli black bean sauce with the cornflour and stock or water until smooth.

4 Add the cornflour mixture to the wok, then return the onion and pepper mixture to the wok and cook, stirring, for 1 minute.

5 Add the noodles and mix lightly. Stir over a medium heat until heated through. Adjust the seasoning. Garnish with spring onions and chillies.

COOK'S TIP: Fermented black beans are whole soya beans preserved in salt and ginger.

Buckwheat Noodles with Smoked Trout

The light, crisp texture of the pak choi balances the earthy flavours of the mushrooms, the buckwheat noodles and the smokiness of the trout.

Serves 4

INGREDIENTS
350 g/12 oz buckwheat noodles
30 ml/2 tbsp vegetable oil
115 g/4 oz fresh shiitake
    mushrooms, quartered
2 garlic cloves, finely chopped
15 ml/1 tbsp grated fresh
    root ginger
225 g/8 oz pak choi
1 spring onion, finely
    sliced diagonally
15 ml/1 tbsp dark sesame oil
30 ml/2 tbsp mirin
30 ml/2 tbsp soy sauce
2 smoked trout, skinned and boned
salt and freshly ground
    black pepper
30 ml/2 tbsp fresh coriander leaves and
    10 ml/2 tsp sesame seeds, toasted,
    to garnish

1 Cook the noodles in a saucepan of boiling water for 7–10 minutes or until they are just tender, following the instructions on the packet.

COOK'S TIP: Mirin is a Japanese sweet rice wine. It has quite a delicate flavour.

2 Meanwhile, heat the oil in a large frying pan. Add the mushrooms and sauté them over a medium heat for 3 minutes. Add the chopped garlic, grated ginger and pak choi and continue to sauté for 2 minutes.

3 Drain the noodles and add them to the mushroom mixture with the spring onion, sesame oil, mirin and soy sauce. Toss and season with salt and pepper to taste.

4 Break the smoked trout into bite-size pieces. Arrange the noodle mixture on individual serving plates. Place the smoked trout on top of the noodles. Garnish the dish with fresh coriander leaves and toasted sesame seeds and serve them immediately.

Noodles with Sun-dried Tomatoes & Prawns

Strongly associated with Mediterranean cooking, sun-dried tomatoes make an inspired addition to this otherwise Eastern-style dish.

Serves 4

INGREDIENTS
350 g/12 oz somen noodles
45 ml/3 tbsp olive oil
20 raw king prawns, peeled and deveined
2 garlic cloves, finely chopped
45–60 ml/3–4 tbsp sun-dried tomato purée
salt and freshly ground black pepper

FOR THE GARNISH
handful of basil leaves
30 ml/2 tbsp sun-dried tomatoes in oil, drained and cut into strips

1 Cook the noodles in a large saucepan of boiling water until tender, following the instructions on the packet. Drain and set aside.

2 Heat half the oil in a large frying pan. Add the prawns and garlic and fry over a medium heat for 3–5 minutes until the prawns turn pink and are firm to the touch.

COOK'S TIP: Ready-made sun-dried tomato purée is readily available, but if you prefer, you can make your own simply by processing bottled sun-dried tomatoes with their oil.

3 Stir in 15 ml/1 tbsp of the sun-dried tomato purée and mix well. Using a slotted spoon, transfer the prawns to a bowl and keep warm.

4 Reheat the oil remaining in the pan. Stir in the rest of the oil with the remaining sun-dried tomato purée. You may need to add a spoonful of water if the mixture is very thick.

5 When the mixture starts to sizzle, toss in the noodles. Add salt and pepper to taste and mix well.

6 Return the prawns to the pan and toss to combine. Serve at once, garnished with the basil and strips of sun-dried tomatoes.

VARIATION: Try processing two anchovy fillets and some capers and adding to the purée.

Noodles with Tuna & Tomato

A scrumptious main meal made from store cupboard ingredients.

Serves 4

INGREDIENTS
45 ml/3 tbsp olive oil
2 garlic cloves, finely chopped
2 dried red chillies, seeded and chopped
1 large red onion, finely sliced
175 g/6 oz canned tuna, drained
115 g/4 oz pitted black olives
400 g/14 oz can plum tomatoes, mashed, or
    400 g/14 oz can chopped tomatoes
30 ml/2 tbsp chopped fresh parsley
350 g/12 oz medium-thick egg noodles
salt and freshly ground black pepper

1 Heat the oil in a large frying pan. Add the garlic and dried chillies and fry for a few seconds. Add the onion and fry, stirring, for about 5 minutes until it softens.

2 Add the tuna and olives to the pan and stir until well mixed. Stir in the tomatoes and any juices. Bring to the boil, season, add the parsley, then lower the heat and simmer gently.

3 Meanwhile, cook the noodles in boiling water until just tender. Drain well, toss with the sauce and serve.

Right: Noodles with Tuna & Tomato (top); Noodles with Mushrooms

Noodles with Mushrooms

The greater the variety of wild mushrooms, the tastier this dish.

Serves 4

INGREDIENTS
350 g/12 oz broad flat egg noodles
45 ml/3 tbsp vegetable oil
115 g/4 oz rindless back or streaky bacon,
    cut into small pieces
225 g/8 oz wild mushrooms, cut in half
115 g/4 oz garlic chives, snipped
225 g/8 oz/1 cup beansprouts
15 ml/1 tbsp oyster sauce
15 ml/1 tbsp soy sauce
salt and freshly ground black pepper

1 Cook the noodles in boiling water until just tender, following the instructions on the packet. Drain, rinse under cold water, drain and set aside.

2 Heat 15 ml/1 tbsp of the oil in a wok or large frying pan. Add the bacon and fry until golden. Set aside.

3 Add the remaining oil to the wok or pan and fry the mushrooms for 3 minutes. Add the garlic chives and beansprouts and fry for 3 minutes, then add the noodles.

4 Season with salt, pepper, oyster sauce and soy sauce. Continue to stir-fry until the noodles are heated through. Sprinkle with the bacon and serve.

Vegetable & Egg Noodle Ribbons

An elegant, colourful dish that makes a superb vegetarian meal.

Serves 4

INGREDIENTS
1 large carrot, peeled
2 courgettes
50 g/2 oz/¼ cup butter
15 ml/1 tbsp olive oil
6 fresh shiitake mushrooms, finely sliced
50 g/2 oz/½ cup frozen peas, thawed
350 g/12 oz broad egg ribbon noodles
10 ml/2 tsp chopped fresh mixed herbs
   (such as marjoram, chives and basil)
salt and freshly ground black pepper
25 g/1 oz Parmesan cheese, to serve (optional)

1 Using a vegetable peeler, carefully slice thin strips from the carrot and courgettes. Heat the butter and oil in a large frying pan. Stir in the carrot and mushrooms; fry for 2 minutes, then add the courgettes and peas. Stir-fry until the courgettes are cooked, but still crisp, season to taste.

2 Meanwhile, cook the noodles in a large saucepan of boiling water until just tender. Drain and tip into a bowl. Add the vegetables and toss to mix. Sprinkle over the herbs and season. Grate or shave over the Parmesan, if using. Toss lightly and serve.

Buckwheat Noodles with Goat's Cheese

The earthy flavour of buckwheat goes well with rocket and cheese.

Serves 4

INGREDIENTS
350 g/12 oz buckwheat noodles
50 g/2 oz/¼ cup butter
2 garlic cloves, finely chopped
4 shallots, sliced
75 g/3 oz/¾ cup hazelnuts, lightly roasted
   and roughly chopped
large handful of rocket leaves
175 g/6 oz goat's cheese
salt and freshly ground black pepper

1 Cook the noodles in a large saucepan of boiling water until just tender, following the instructions on the packet. Drain well and set aside. Heat the butter in a large frying pan. Add the garlic and shallots and cook for 2–3 minutes, stirring all the time, until the shallots are soft.

2 Add the hazelnuts and fry for about 1 minute. Add the rocket leaves and, when they start to wilt, toss in the noodles and heat through. Season with salt and pepper to taste. Crumble in the goat's cheese and serve immediately.

Right: Vegetable & Egg Noodle Ribbons (top); Buckwheat Noodles with Goat's Cheese

Noodles with Asparagus & Saffron Sauce

This dish combines summer vegetables in a fragrant saffron cream.

Serves 4

INGREDIENTS
450 g/1 lb young asparagus
pinch of saffron threads
25 g/1 oz/2 tbsp butter
2 shallots, finely chopped
30 ml/2 tbsp white wine
250 ml/8 fl oz/1 cup
   double cream
grated rind and juice of ½ lemon
115 g/4 oz/1 cup peas
350 g/12 oz somen noodles
½ bunch fresh chervil, roughly chopped
salt and freshly ground
   black pepper
grated Parmesan cheese, to serve (optional)

2 Melt the butter in a saucepan, add the shallots and cook over a low heat for 3 minutes until soft. Add the white wine, cream and saffron infusion.

3 Bring to the boil, reduce the heat and simmer gently for 5 minutes or until the sauce thickens to a coating consistency. Add the grated lemon rind and juice, with salt and pepper to taste.

4 Bring a large saucepan of lightly salted water to the boil. Blanch the asparagus tips, scoop them out and add them to the sauce, then cook the peas and short asparagus rounds in the boiling water until just tender. Scoop them out and add to the sauce.

1 Cut off the asparagus tips (make them about 5 cm/2 in in length), then slice the remaining spears into short rounds. Place the saffron in a cup and pour over 30 ml/2 tbsp boiling water. Leave to steep.

5 Cook the noodles in the same water until just tender, following the instructions on the packet. Drain, place in a wide pan and pour the sauce over the top.

6 Toss the noodles with the sauce and vegetables, adding the chervil and more salt and pepper if needed. Finally, sprinkle with the grated Parmesan, if using, and serve.

COOK'S TIP: You can use fresh or frozen peas for this dish.

Seafood Laksa

For a special occasion serve this dish of creamy rice noodles in a spicy coconut-flavoured soup, topped with seafood.

Serves 4

INGREDIENTS
4 red chillies, seeded and
    roughly chopped
1 onion, roughly chopped
1 piece *blachan*, the size of a stock cube
1 lemon grass stalk, chopped
1 small piece fresh root ginger, peeled and
    roughly chopped
6 macadamia nuts or almonds
60 ml/4 tbsp vegetable oil
5 ml/1 tsp paprika
5 ml/1 tsp ground turmeric
475 ml/16 fl oz/2 cups stock or water
600 ml/1 pint/2½ cups coconut milk
Thai fish sauce *(nam pla)*, to taste
12 king prawns, peeled and deveined
8 scallops
225 g/8 oz prepared squid,
    cut into rings
350 g/12 oz rice vermicelli or rice noodles,
    soaked in warm water until soft
    and drained
salt and freshly ground
    black pepper
lime halves, to serve

FOR THE GARNISH
¼ cucumber, cut into matchsticks
2 red chillies, seeded and finely sliced
30 ml/2 tbsp fresh mint leaves
30 ml/2 tbsp fried shallots
    or onions

1 In a blender or food processor, process the chillies, onion, *blachan*, lemon grass, ginger and nuts until smooth in texture.

2 Heat 45 ml/3 tbsp of the oil in a large saucepan. Add the chilli paste and fry for 6 minutes. Stir in the spices and fry for about 2 minutes more.

3 Add the stock or water and the coconut milk to the pan. Bring to the boil, reduce the heat and simmer gently for 15–20 minutes. Season to taste with fish sauce.

4 Season the seafood with salt and pepper. Heat the remaining oil in a frying pan, add the seafood and fry quickly for 2–3 minutes until cooked.

COOK'S TIP: *Blachan* is strongly flavoured dried shrimp paste. It is sold in small blocks and you will find it in Oriental supermarkets.

5 Add the noodles to the soup and heat through. Divide among individual serving bowls. Place the fried seafood on top, then garnish with the cucumber, chillies, fresh mint leaves and fried shallots or onions. Serve with the lime halves.

Chiang Mai Noodle Soup

Named after the Thai city of Chiang Mai, this delicious noodle soup has Burmese origins and is the Thai equivalent of the Malaysian "laksa".

Serves 4–6

INGREDIENTS
600 ml/1 pint/2½ cups coconut milk
30 ml/2 tbsp ready-made red curry paste
5 ml/1 tsp ground turmeric
450 g/1 lb chicken thighs, boned and cut into
  bite-size chunks
600 ml/1 pint/2½ cups Chicken Stock
60 ml/4 tbsp Thai fish sauce *(nam pla)*
15 ml/1 tbsp dark soy sauce
juice of ½–1 lime
450 g/1 lb fresh egg noodles, blanched
  briefly in boiling water
salt and freshly ground
  black pepper

FOR THE GARNISH
3 spring onions, chopped
4 red chillies, chopped
4 shallots, chopped
60 ml/4 tbsp sliced pickled mustard
  leaves, rinsed
30 ml/2 tbsp sliced garlic, fried
fresh coriander leaves
4 fried noodle nests (optional)

1 Place about one-third of the coconut milk in a large saucepan and slowly bring it to the boil, stirring frequently with a wooden spoon until it separates.

2 Add the curry paste and ground turmeric, stir to mix completely and cook until fragrant.

3 Add the chicken and stir-fry for about 2 minutes, ensuring that all the chunks are coated with the paste.

4 Add the remaining coconut milk, the chicken stock, fish sauce and soy sauce. Season with salt and pepper to taste. Simmer gently for 7–10 minutes. Remove from the heat and stir in the lime juice.

5 Reheat the noodles in boiling water, drain and divide among individual bowls. Divide the chicken among the bowls and ladle in the hot soup. Top each serving with a few of each of the garnishes.

COOK'S TIP: Pickled mustard leaves can be found in most good Oriental stores.

Snapper, Tomato & Tamarind Noodle Soup

Tamarind gives this light, fragrant noodle soup a slightly sour taste.

Serves 4

INGREDIENTS

2 litres/3½ pints/8 cups water
1 kg/2¼ lb red snapper or other red fish
    such as mullet
1 onion, sliced
50 g/2 oz tamarind pods
15 ml/1 tbsp Thai fish sauce *(nam pla)*
15 ml/1 tbsp sugar
30 ml/2 tbsp vegetable oil
2 garlic cloves, finely chopped
2 lemon grass stalks, very
    finely chopped
4 ripe tomatoes, roughly chopped
30 ml/2 tbsp yellow bean paste
225 g/8 oz rice vermicelli, soaked in warm
    water until soft
115 g/4 oz/½ cup beansprouts
8–10 fresh basil or mint sprigs
25 g/1 oz/¼ cup ground
    roasted peanuts
salt and freshly ground
    black pepper

1 Bring the water to the boil in a large saucepan. Lower the heat and add the whole fish and sliced onion, with 2.5 ml/½ tsp salt. Simmer gently until the fish is cooked through.

2 Remove the fish from the stock and set aside. Add the tamarind, fish sauce and sugar to the stock. Cook for 5 minutes, then strain the stock into a large jug or bowl.

3 When the fish is cool enough to handle, carefully remove all the bones, keeping the flesh in big pieces.

4 Heat the oil in a large frying pan. Add the garlic and lemon grass and fry for a few seconds. Stir in the tomatoes and yellow bean paste. Cook gently for 5–7 minutes until the tomatoes are soft.

5 Add the stock, bring back to a simmer and adjust the seasoning.

6 Drain the vermicelli. Plunge them into a saucepan of boiling water for a few minutes, then drain them again and divide them among individual serving bowls.

7 Add the beansprouts, fish and basil or mint. Sprinkle with the ground peanuts. Top up each bowl with the hot soup and serve immediately.

COOK'S TIP: Tamarind pods are the seed cases of a tropical tree. Buy them from Oriental stores.

Chicken & Noodle Soup

A well-flavoured stock is vital to the success of this hearty soup, which uses buckwheat noodles, widely enjoyed in Japan.

Serves 4

INGREDIENTS
225 g/8 oz skinless, boneless chicken breasts
120 ml/4 fl oz/½ cup soy sauce
15 ml/1 tbsp saké
1 litre/1¾ pints/4 cups Chicken Stock
2 pieces young leeks
175 g/6 oz spinach leaves
300 g/11 oz buckwheat or soba noodles
toasted sesame seeds, to garnish

1 Slice the chicken diagonally into bite-size pieces. Combine the soy sauce and saké in a saucepan and bring to a simmer. Add the chicken and cook gently for about 3 minutes until it is tender. Keep warm.

2 Bring the stock to the boil in another saucepan. Slice the leeks into 2.5 cm/1 in lengths, then add to the stock and simmer for 3 minutes, then add the spinach. Remove from the heat, but keep warm.

3 Cook the noodles in a large saucepan of boiling water until just tender, following the instructions on the packet.

4 Drain the noodles and divide them among individual serving bowls. Ladle the hot soup into the bowls, then add a portion of chicken to each. Serve at once, sprinkled with the toasted sesame seeds.

Udon Pot

Brimming with flavour, this soup would make a fine starter or light lunch.

Serves 4

INGREDIENTS
350 g/12 oz dried udon noodles
1 large carrot, cut into bite-size chunks
225 g/8 oz chicken breasts or thighs, skinned
    and cut into bite-size pieces
8 raw king prawns, peeled and deveined
4–6 Chinese cabbage leaves, cut into
    short strips
8 shiitake mushrooms, stems removed
50 g/2 oz/½ cup mangetouts,
    topped and tailed
1.5 litres/2½ pints/6¼ cups Chicken Stock or
    instant bonito stock
30 ml/2 tbsp mirin
soy sauce, to taste
1 bunch spring onions, finely chopped,
    30 ml/2 tbsp grated fresh root ginger,
    lemon wedges and extra soy sauce, to serve

1 Cook the noodles until just tender, following the instructions on the packet. Drain, rinse under cold water and drain again. Blanch the carrot in boiling water for 1 minute, then drain.

2 Spoon the noodles and carrot into a large saucepan or flameproof casserole. Arrange the chicken, prawns, and vegetables on top.

3 Bring the stock to the boil in a saucepan. Add the mirin and soy sauce to taste. Pour over the noodles. Cover, bring to the boil over a moderate heat, then simmer gently for 5–6 minutes until all the ingredients are cooked. Serve topped with chopped spring onions, grated ginger, lemon wedges and a sprinkling of soy sauce.

Hanoi Beef & Noodle Soup

Millions of North Vietnamese eat this fragrant soup for breakfast.

Serves 4–6

INGREDIENTS
1 onion
1.3–1.6 kg/3–3½ lb beef shank
  with bones
2.5 cm/1 in piece fresh root ginger
1 star anise
1 bay leaf
2 cloves
2.5 ml/½ tsp fennel seeds
1 piece cassia bark or cinnamon stick
3 litres/5 pints/13 cups water
Thai fish sauce *(nam pla)*, to taste
juice of 1 lime
150 g/5 oz fillet steak
450 g/1 lb fresh flat rice noodles
salt and freshly ground
  black pepper

FOR THE ACCOMPANIMENTS
1 small red onion, sliced
  into rings
115 g/4 oz/½ cup beansprouts
2 red chillies, seeded and sliced
2 spring onions, finely sliced
handful of fresh coriander leaves
lime wedges

1 Preheat the grill to high. Cut the onion in half. Grill under a high heat, cut side up, until the exposed sides have become caramelized and are a deep brown colour. Set aside.

2 Cut the beef shank into large chunks and place with the bones in a large saucepan or stock pot. Add the caramelized onion with the ginger, star anise, bay leaf, cloves, fennel seeds and cassia bark or cinnamon stick.

3 Add the water, bring to the boil, reduce the heat and simmer gently for 2–3 hours, skimming occasionally.

4 Using a slotted spoon, remove the meat from the stock; when cool enough to handle, cut into small pieces, discarding the bones. Strain the stock and return to the pan together with the meat. Bring back to the boil and season with the fish sauce and lime juice.

5 Slice the fillet steak very thinly and chill until required. Place the accompaniments in separate bowls. Cook the noodles in a large saucepan of boiling water until just tender, following the instructions on the packet, then drain.

6 Divide the noodles among individual serving bowls. Arrange the thinly sliced steak on top and pour over the hot stock. Serve, offering the accompaniments separately so that each person may garnish their soup as they like.

49

Cheat's Shark's Fin Soup

In China shark's fin soup is a renowned delicacy. In this subtly flavoured vegetarian version, cellophane noodles, cut into short lengths, mimic shark's fin needles.

Serves 4–6

INGREDIENTS
4 dried Chinese mushrooms
25 ml/1½ tbsp dried wood ears
115 g/4 oz cellophane noodles
30 ml/2 tbsp vegetable oil
2 carrots, cut into fine strips
115 g/4 oz canned bamboo shoots,
    rinsed, drained and cut into
    fine strips
1 litre/1¾ pints/4 cups light vegetable stock
15 ml/1 tbsp soy sauce
15 ml/1 tbsp arrowroot or
    potato flour
30 ml/2 tbsp water
1 egg white, beaten (optional)
5 ml/1 tsp sesame oil
salt and freshly ground
    black pepper
2 spring onions, finely chopped,
    to garnish
Chinese red vinegar,
    to serve (optional)

1 Soak the Chinese mushrooms and wood ears separately in warm water for 20 minutes. Drain well.

2 Remove and discard the mushroom stems and thinly slice the caps. Cut the wood ears into fine strips, discarding any particularly hard bits.

3 Soak the noodles in hot water until soft. Drain and cut into short lengths. Leave until required.

4 Heat the oil in a large saucepan. Add the Chinese mushrooms and stir-fry for 2 minutes. Add the wood ears, stir-fry for 2 minutes, then stir in the carrots, bamboo shoots and noodles.

5 Add the vegetable stock to the pan. Bring to the boil, reduce the heat and simmer gently for 15–20 minutes. Season with soy sauce, salt and freshly ground black pepper.

6 Blend the arrowroot or potato flour with a little water. Pour into the soup, stirring to prevent lumps from forming as the soup continues to simmer.

COOK'S TIP: Wood ears are a popular Chinese fungi.

7 Remove the pan from the heat. Stir in the egg white, if using, so that it sets to form small threads in the hot soup. Stir in the sesame oil, then pour the soup into individual bowls. Sprinkle each portion with chopped spring onions and offer the Chinese red vinegar separately, if using.

Sichuan Noodles with Sesame Sauce

These noodles, tossed with a hot, sweet and sour sauce, are served with a separate bowl of crisp, fresh-tasting vegetables.

Serves 3–4

INGREDIENTS
450 g/1 lb fresh or 225 g/8 oz dried
    egg noodles
½ cucumber, sliced lengthways, seeded
    and diced
4–6 spring onions
1 bunch radishes, about 115 g/4 oz
225 g/8 oz mooli, peeled
115 g/4 oz/½ cup beansprouts, rinsed then
    left in iced water and drained
60 ml/4 tbsp groundnut or sunflower oil
2 garlic cloves, crushed
45 ml/3 tbsp toasted sesame paste
15 ml/1 tbsp sesame oil
15 ml/1 tbsp light soy sauce
5–10 ml/1–2 tsp chilli sauce, to taste
15 ml/1 tbsp rice vinegar
120 ml/4 fl oz/½ cup vegetable
    stock or water
5 ml/1 tsp sugar, or to taste
salt and freshly ground black pepper
roasted peanuts or cashew nuts,
    to garnish

1 If using fresh noodles, cook them in boiling water for 1 minute, then drain well. Rinse in fresh water and drain again. If using dried noodles, cook them following the instructions on the packet, draining and rinsing them as for fresh noodles.

2 Sprinkle the cucumber with salt, leave for 15 minutes, rinse well, then drain and pat dry on kitchen paper. Place in a large salad bowl.

3 Cut the spring onions into fine shreds. Cut the radishes in half and slice finely. Coarsely grate the mooli using a mandolin or food processor. Add all the vegetables to the diced cucumber and toss gently.

COOK'S TIP: Chinese sesame paste is available from Oriental stores.

4 Heat half the oil in a wok or frying pan and stir-fry the noodles for about 1 minute. Using a slotted spoon, transfer the noodles to a large serving bowl and keep warm.

5 Add the remaining oil to the wok. When it is hot, fry the garlic to flavour the oil. Remove from the heat.

6 Stir in the sesame paste, with the sesame oil, soy and chilli sauces, vinegar and stock or water. Add a little sugar and season to taste. Warm through over a gentle heat. Do not overheat or the sauce will thicken too much. Pour over the noodles and toss well. Garnish with peanuts or cashews. Serve with the vegetables.

53

Toasted Noodles with Vegetables

Slightly crisp noodle cakes topped with vegetables make a superb dish.

Serves 4

INGREDIENTS
175 g/6 oz dried egg vermicelli
15 ml/1 tbsp vegetable oil
2 garlic cloves, finely chopped
115 g/4 oz/1 cup baby corn cobs
115 g/4 oz/1 cup halved fresh
    shiitake mushrooms
3 celery sticks, sliced
1 carrot, diagonally sliced
115 g/4 oz/1 cup mangetouts
75 g/3 oz/¾ cup sliced, drained, canned
    bamboo shoots
15 ml/1 tbsp cornflour
15 ml/1 tbsp cold water
15 ml/1 tbsp dark soy sauce
5 ml/1 tsp caster sugar
300 ml/½ pint/1¼ cups vegetable stock
salt and freshly ground white pepper
spring onion curls, to garnish

1 Bring a saucepan of water to the boil. Add the egg vermicelli and cook until just tender, following the instructions on the packet. Drain, refresh under cold water, drain again, then dry thoroughly on kitchen paper.

2 Heat 2.5 ml/½ tsp oil in a non-stick wok or frying pan. When it is very hot, spread half the noodles over the base. Fry for 2–3 minutes until lightly toasted.

3 Carefully turn the noodles over (they stick together like a cake), fry the other side, then slide on to a heated serving plate. Repeat with the remaining noodles to make two cakes. Keep warm.

4 Heat the remaining oil in the clean wok or pan, then fry the garlic for a few seconds. Halve the corn cobs lengthways, add to the pan with the mushrooms, then stir-fry for 3 minutes, adding a little water, if needed, to prevent the mixture burning.

5 Add the celery, carrot, mangetouts and bamboo shoots and stir-fry for 2 minutes or until the vegetables are tender-crisp.

6 Mix the cornflour to a thin paste with the water. Add the mixture to the pan with the soy sauce, sugar and stock. Cook, stirring, until the sauce thickens. Season with salt and white pepper.

7 Place the vegetable mixture on top of the noodle cakes, garnish with the spring onion curls and serve immediately. Each noodle cake serves two people.

VARIATION: Other vegetables can also be used. Broccoli, beansprouts and peppers would all work well.

Vegetarian Fried Noodles

No worries about this tasty vegetarian dish being short on protein as it includes beancurd and is garnished with egg omelette strips.

Serves 4

INGREDIENTS
2 eggs
5 ml/1 tsp chilli powder
5 ml/1 tsp ground turmeric
60 ml/4 tbsp vegetable oil
1 large onion, finely sliced
2 red chillies, seeded and finely sliced
15 ml/1 tbsp soy sauce
2 large cooked potatoes, cut into
    small cubes
6 pieces fried beancurd, sliced
225 g/8 oz/1 cup beansprouts
115 g/4 oz/¾ cup green beans, blanched
350 g/12 oz fresh thick egg noodles
salt and freshly ground black pepper
sliced spring onions, to garnish

1 Beat the eggs lightly, then strain them into a bowl. Heat a lightly greased omelette pan or wok. Pour in half of the egg to cover the bottom of the pan thinly. When the egg is just set, turn the omelette over and fry the other side briefly.

2 Slide the omelette on to a plate, blot with kitchen paper, roll up and cut into narrow strips. Make a second omelette in the same way and slice. Set the omelette strips aside for the garnish.

3 In a cup, mix together the chilli powder and turmeric. Form a paste by stirring in a little water.

4 Heat the oil in a wok or frying pan. Fry the onion until soft. Reduce the heat and add the chilli paste, chillies and soy sauce. Fry for 2–3 minutes.

5 Add the potatoes and fry for about 2 minutes, mixing well with the chillies. Add the beancurd, then the beansprouts, green beans and noodles.

COOK'S TIP: Always be very careful when handling chillies. Keep your hands away from your eyes as chillies will sting them. Wash your hands thoroughly after touching chillies.

6 Gently stir-fry until the noodles are evenly coated and heated through. Take care not to break up the potatoes or the beancurd. Season with salt and pepper. Serve hot, garnished with the omelette strips and spring onion slices.

Indian Mee Goreng

A truly international vegetarian noodle dish combining Indian, Chinese and Western ingredients.

Serves 4–6

INGREDIENTS
450 g/1 lb fresh egg noodles
115 g/4 oz fried beancurd or
     150 g/5 oz firm beancurd
60–90 ml/4–6 tbsp vegetable oil
2 eggs
30 ml/2 tbsp water
1 onion, sliced
1 garlic clove, crushed
15 ml/1 tbsp light soy sauce
30–45 ml/2–3 tbsp tomato ketchup
15 ml/1 tbsp chilli sauce,
     or to taste
1 large cooked potato, diced
4 spring onions, shredded
1–2 green chillies, seeded and finely
     sliced (optional)

2 If using fried beancurd, cut each cube in half, refresh it in a pan of boiling water, then drain well. If using plain beancurd, cut into cubes. Heat 30 ml/2 tbsp of the oil in a large frying pan and fry until brown, then lift it out and set aside.

3 In a bowl, beat the eggs with the water and seasoning. Add to the oil in the frying pan and cook without stirring until set. Flip the omelette over, cook the other side, then slide it out of the pan, roll up and slice thinly.

4 Heat the remaining oil in a wok and fry the onion and garlic for 2–3 minutes. Add the noodles, soy sauce, ketchup and chilli sauce. Toss well over medium heat for 2 minutes.

1 Bring a large saucepan of water to the boil, add the fresh egg noodles and cook them for just 2 minutes. Drain and immediately rinse the noodles under cold water to halt cooking. Drain again and set aside.

5 Add the diced potato. Reserve a few spring onion shreds for the garnish and stir the rest into the noodles with the chilli, if using, and the beancurd.

6 When hot, stir in the omelette strips. Serve on a hot platter, garnished with the reserved spring onion shreds.

COOK'S TIP: Beancurd, also known as tofu, is made from soya beans. It is available in several forms, including soft, firm, silken, grilled, dried and fried.

Thai Noodle Salad

The addition of coconut milk and sesame oil gives an unusual nutty flavour to the dressing for this colourful noodle salad.

Serves 4–6

INGREDIENTS

350 g/12 oz somen noodles
1 large carrot, cut into thin strips
1 bunch asparagus, trimmed and cut into
    4 cm/1½ in lengths
1 red pepper, seeded and cut into
    fine strips
115 g/4 oz/1 cup mangetouts, topped,
    tailed and halved
115 g/4 oz/1 cup baby corn cobs,
    halved lengthways
115 g/4 oz/½ cup beansprouts
115 g/4 oz can water chestnuts, drained and
    finely sliced
1 lime, cut into wedges, 50 g/2 oz/½ cup
    roughly chopped roasted peanuts, and
    fresh coriander leaves, to garnish

FOR THE DRESSING

45 ml/3 tbsp roughly torn fresh basil
75 ml/5 tbsp roughly chopped fresh mint
250 ml/8 fl oz/1 cup coconut milk
30 ml/2 tbsp dark sesame oil
15 ml/1 tbsp grated fresh root ginger
2 garlic cloves, finely chopped
juice of 1 lime
2 spring onions, finely chopped
salt and cayenne pepper

VARIATION: Shredded omelette or sliced hard-boiled eggs are also popular garnishes for this salad.

1 To make the dressing, combine the basil, mint, coconut milk, sesame oil, ginger, garlic, lime juice and spring onions in a bowl and mix well. Season to taste with salt and cayenne pepper.

2 Cook the noodles in a saucepan of boiling water until just tender, following the instructions on the packet. Drain, rinse under cold running water and drain again.

3 Cook all the vegetables separately in a saucepan of boiling, lightly salted water until tender but still crisp. Drain, plunge them immediately into cold water and drain again.

4 Toss the noodles, vegetables and dressing together to combine. Arrange on individual serving plates and garnish with the lime wedges, peanuts and coriander leaves.

Thamin Lethok

This attractive dish of noodles, rice and vegetables is the Burmese way of dealing with leftovers, and very successful it is too.

Serves 6

INGREDIENTS
175 g/6 oz/scant 1 cup long grain rice
1–2 red chillies, seeded and roughly chopped
1 small onion, roughly chopped
15 ml/1 tbsp vegetable oil
350 g/12 oz potatoes, diced (optional)
115 g/4 oz egg noodles, soaked for
    30 minutes in cold water to cover
115 g/4 oz rice noodles, soaked for at least
    10 minutes in cold water to cover
50 g/2 oz cellophane noodles
    (or increase either of the above)
225 g/8 oz spinach leaves
175 g/6 oz/¾ cup beansprouts
25 ml/1½ tbsp tamarind pulp or concentrate,
    soaked in 200 ml/7 fl oz/scant 1 cup
    warm water, or 6 lemon wedges
salt

FOR THE ACCOMPANIMENTS
1 very small onion, thinly sliced
3 spring onions, finely shredded
1 onion, sliced and deep-fried until crisp
50 g/2 oz cellophane noodles, fried until crisp
25 g/1 oz/3 tbsp chick-peas, dry roasted
    and pounded (optional)
3 dried chillies, dry-fried and pounded
fresh coriander leaves (optional)

1 Bring a large pan of water to the boil, add the rice and cook for 12–15 minutes until tender. Drain, tip into a bowl and set aside.

2 In a mortar, pound the fresh chillies with the onion. Heat the oil in a small frying pan, add the mixture and fry for 2–3 minutes. Stir into the cooked rice and leave to cool.

3 Cook the potatoes, if using, in boiling, salted water for about 8–10 minutes until just tender; drain and set aside. Drain the noodles and cook them in separate pans of boiling, salted water until tender, following the instructions on the packet. Drain, refresh under cold water and drain.

4 Put the spinach into a large pan with just the water that clings to the leaves after washing. Cover the pan and cook for 2 minutes until starting to wilt. Drain well. Cook the beansprouts in the same way. Leave both to cool.

5 Arrange the flavoured rice, potato cubes, noodles, spinach and beansprouts attractively on a large serving platter.

6 Set out the range of prepared accompaniments. Strain the tamarind juice, if using, into a jug or put the lemon wedges on a plate. Each guest takes a little of whichever main ingredients they fancy, adds some accompaniments and drizzles over a little tamarind juice or a squeeze of lemon juice to taste.

This edition is published by Hermes House

Hermes House is an imprint of Anness Publishing Ltd
Hermes House, 88–89 Blackfriars Road, London SE1 8HA
tel. 020 7401 2077; fax 020 7633 9499; info@anness.com

© Anness Publishing Ltd 2001, 2003

A CIP catalogue record for this book is available from the British Library.

Publisher: Joanna Lorenz
Editor: Valerie Ferguson
Series Designer: Bobbie Colgate Stone
Designer: Andrew Heath
Production Controller: Joanna King

Recipes contributed by: Kit Chan,
Deh-Ta Hsuing, Kathy Man, Sallie Morris.

Photography: William Adams-Lingwood, Micki Dowie,
Janine Hosegood, Thomas Odulate.

Previously published as *Great Noodle Dishes*

Notes:
For all recipes, quantities are given in both metric and imperial measures and,
where appropriate, measures are also given in standard cups and spoons.
Follow one set, but not a mixture, because they are not interchangeable.
Standard spoon and cup measures are level.
1 tsp = 5 ml   1 tbsp = 15 ml
1 cup = 250 ml/8 fl oz
Australian standard tablespoons are 20 ml.
Australian readers should use 3 tsp in place of
1 tbsp for measuring small quantities of gelatine, cornflour, salt etc.
Medium eggs are used unless otherwise stated.

1 3 5 7 9 10 8 6 4 2